A Day
Within
Days

To the memory of my father Wang Huaiyi

A Day Within Days

Liu Hongbin

Here from Elsewhere

AB

First published in 2006 by Ambit Books,
17 Priory Gardens, London N6 5QY, UK
Publisher: Martin Bax
© 2006 by Liu Hongbin
Cover image © 2006 by Vanessa Jackson
The moral rights of the author and artist are asserted in
accordance with the Copyright, Designs and Patent Act, 1988

All rights reserved. No part of this publication may be reproduced,
stored in a retrieval system, or transmitted, in any form or by any means,
electronic, mechanical, photocopying, recording or otherwise without the prior
permission in writing of the publisher.

ISBN 0-900055-10-3
ISBN 978-0-900055-10-2

Designed by John Morgan studio
Cover image by Vanessa Jackson
Printed in Great Britain by The Lavenham Press
Distributed by Central Books
The publisher acknowledges the financial assistance of Arts Council England

Acknowledgements

Some of these poems first appeared in the following journals and anthologies: *Agenda, Another Province: New Chinese Writing from London* (Lambeth Chinese Community Association, 1994), *Banned Poetry* (Index on Censorship, 1997), *Captured Voices* (Victor Gollancz, 1999; Indigo, 2000), *Casablanca, China Now* (London), *The Fourth World Review, The Independent, The Independent on Sunday, IPI Report, PEN International*. The author gratefully acknowledges the editors.

'Voice' was broadcast on BBC Radio 3. Extracts of 'Sparrow' were broadcast on BBC2's Newsnight, and 'Words' on CBS News' 'Under Fire' programme. An extract from 'A Day Within Days' was broadcast on Voice of America and Radio Free Asia's Chinese service.

'Spirit of the Sea' was set to music by Joyce Bee Tuan Koh and performed at Conway Hall, Red Lion Square, London, for the Sound International Concert 1996.

The author thanks Human Rights Watch, New York, for a Hellman / Hammett Award in 1997 and 1999; PEN Emergency Fund; the Trustees of Hawthornden Castle, Lothian, for a resident Fellowship (1999); the British Centre for Literary Translation for a post as translator in residence (1999); the Royal Literary Fund for a timely grant (2000); and the Institute of English Studies, University of London, for a Visiting Research Fellowship (2004–05). Thanks also to Doris Lessing, Anita Money and Rita Auden for support during difficult times, and to David Hawkes for reading the entire manuscript and making valuable suggestions.

All the poems in this collection have been translated from Chinese into English by the author with Peter Porter, except: 'A Hunting Song in the Forest' (with Jason Brooks); 'An Autumn Leaf', 'Birthday Card, 1990', 'Door', 'Only One Way', 'So, Let Us Part', 'The Man and the Sea', 'Waiting', 'Within the Colour of Night' (with Ione Meyer); 'Boyhood' (with D.J. Enright); 'Spirit of the Sea' (John Cayley); 'Voice' (Elaine Feinstein); 'Who Are You?' (with Peter Porter and Jason Brooks). Grateful thanks to all those who helped with the translations.

Introduction

That so fine a poet as Liu Hongbin has been a victim of our Age of Displacement and Exile is not the most important thing about him. Despite having been forced to leave China after the events of Tiananmen Square in 1989 and after living in exile in the West (chiefly in Britain), he remains a poet first and foremost, a master of his language secondly, and only lastly someone persecuted by the politics of his nation. His first poems after leaving China in 1989 were preoccupied, naturally enough, in presenting in rhetorical terms the outrageous conduct of China's rulers. However, even in the poems after leaving China – despite a sense of outrage and loss – there is nothing overtly political at work; a proper sense of historical perspective is always present.

Liu studied English in his native city of Qingdao (Tsingtao), and is well versed in the tradition of English literature, especially poetry and particularly poetry in the 20th century. This is not to suggest that Liu's work derives in any way from English practice, only that being truthful verse *sui generis*, it can be reborn in English. Translation may be an unconscious form of treachery, but it instinctively reacts to good work by desiring to remake it in its own language at an equivalent intensity of commitment.

As one of the English-speaking poets who have worked with Liu in attempting to bring his verse to life in our tongue, I should confess, and perhaps apologise, for our practice. I cannot read a single Chinese character and I understand the tradition of classical Chinese poetry only through reading it in English verse. However, Liu himself bridges the essential gap between our cultures. He outlines the poem's essential gift and portrays it in English; he speaks of its form in Chinese and he trusts us to find a manner of presentation, which may include rhetorical parallels between the two languages. From then on it is his genius and our understanding of English poetry that produces the poem, resulting here in a collection of work of prime and original force.

Peter Porter
London, May 2006

Contents

Boyhood *8*
A Hunting Song in the Forest *10*
Images *12*
Red Wine *13*
An Autumn Leaf / A Football *14*
Within the Colour of Night *15*
So, Let Us Part *16*
Waiting *17*
Spirit of the Sea *18*
The Man and the Sea *19*
Rubik's Cube *20*
You Predicted my Destiny *22*
Alleyway *24*
Voice *25*
Door *26*
Who Are You? *28*
To C.J. *30*
A Consultation / Birthday Card, 1990 *32*
In the Bathroom *33*
Learning a New Language *34*
Words *35*
Chance / Discovery *36*
Boarding the Boat of Death Half Way *37*
Desire Hotel *38*
A Prayer / I See *39*
The Unfamiliar Customs House *40*
A Day Within Days *42*
Valediction *48*
Listening to Chinese Music *50*
Only One Way *51*
Insomnia *52*
Standing at the Doors of Dusk *53*
At Hawthornden Castle *54*
This Poem *55*

少年

從鼻孔裊出
淚水打濕的煙
灰風擦洗著酒杯
心
卻想躲進混沌

泡在酒裡的心
痙攣地吻著我的唇
我們默默地談著
話
別人聽不懂

我要在藍霧中
找到未被酒澆滅的太陽
清澈的風在光中吹著哨
我
晨霧中一個無知的頑童

Boyhood

Smoke, tear-damped, curls
from the nostrils.
A grey wind wiping clean the wine glass;
but my heart
wishes to withdraw into obscurity.

My heart, soaked in wine,
is convulsed as it kisses my lips,
we utter
words
which others do not understand.

Through the blue haze, I look for
that sun not yet doused with wine.
A limpid wind whistles in the sunlight.
Myself
an innocent child in the morning mist.

A Hunting Song in the Forest

On a pitch-black night
My ghostly spectre
Lies quietly in a solitary tomb beside a forest path.
My flesh, my bones
Strewn outside among the scattered stones and weeds.
I am alone,
Will-o'-the-wisp, now white now blue, my sole companion.

One night not long ago,
Rifle in hand,
I slid deep into the forest.
My prey,
Stealthy, tries desperately to escape my clutches.
My eyes,
Gradually veiled by the nightly curtain.

A wave of dejection comes over me.
Bursting into a fury,
I chase after my prey with all my might.
I lose track of time
And the darkness creeps up on me.
My life
Is coveted by the monsters and vipers of the night.

On that pitch-black night,
My warm blood
Is greedily sucked dry.
My corpse is wolfed down and gnawed.
My thoughts
Turn into blue smoke, dissipating.

My immortal soul contemplates:
The hunt for the prey,
Aren't sharp eyes all that are needed?

For the chase,
Isn't reckless courage all that is needed?
For the capture,
Isn't a momentary impulse all that is needed?

I lie quietly in the forest.
My former body,
Scattered around, unable to stand.
The wind rustles through the forest,
Moaning deeply.

The hunting rifle at my side
Also pours out its complaint.

On a pitch-black night,
My ghostly spectre
Lies quietly in a solitary tomb beside a forest path.
My flesh, my bones,
Strewn outside among the scattered stones and weeds.
I am alone,
Will-o'-the-wisp, now white now blue, my sole companion.

Images

A tailor's scissors
Cut clothes.

A blade of light
Slits the nightly velvet.

A blind man breaks through the fog
To go walking.

Red Wine

In the glass, there are ripples of passion.
In the wine, there is no desolate moon.
To your health, friend
Pour the wine, ruby red
To melt the snow encrusted in the heart.

An Autumn Leaf

With the autumn wind fluttering and drifting down,
Squashed to dust and mud to enrich the earth;
Or picked up by an affectionate young girl under the tree,
Slipping it into her scrapbook of years.

A Football

A football abandoned
Is covered by silently fallen snow.
In the morning, the aged have not come out to stroll as usual;
Only a crowd of children snowman-making.

Within the Colour of Night

The sea in the mood for love kisses the shore,
Marking a meandering line on the beach.
Waves rush towards the reef,
An expanse of white lotus sprays mist in the air.
A sailor amid gusts of wind and rain lifts anchor,
Hoisting the sail of confidence.
A young girl on the shore weaves the silk threads of tenacity and bravery,
And makes a garland for his safe return.

31 March 1982

So, Let Us Part

The grove still stands there.
You are leaving now:
Drops of wishes glistening
Fall from your lips,
Echoing within the enchanted grove.

A path woven in moonlight floats in all directions.

The homing pigeon sets off.
In turn, woods, bush fire and coal strata are changing places.
The sun of hours steers my boat
Out of the harbour's dawn.

The darkened grove vanishes.
The burning sky is like a ship sailing with the wind.

Where the mist obscures,
I remember
You never once embraced me.
At that very moment, the rush of the wind through the trees,
Rumbling like the flood,
Beats against our rocking ark.

You are leaving now.
Before the flood of night descends,
I wish you well.
Take my torch please – it will light the way.
So, let us part.

Waiting

The world is breathing in green.
Bristling lawn has opened its pores.
On the bed there is a pool of green light,
I lie awaiting your return.

The sun, a mischievous boy,
Holding up moistened red and blue handkerchiefs,
Erects a ceiling.

The wood is quietly stretching out its newly born arms,
Embracing the little bird hiding its red tongue.
Under this gloomy umbrella
The bird is unwilling to sing his lonely solo.

Angels dressed in white silk showering silver coins
Dance in gracefully.
It is evening.

1984

Spirit of the Sea

That song has been drowned.
Within the rushing waves, the surging, glancing light,
I have found my voice.

That life has been destroyed.
On a half-submerged rock, torn by the waves of the sea,
I have rediscovered my origins.

I want to build a new life.

Sea-gulls, nestling in light mist –
the wings of dreams in air –
time is a flock of gulls, taking wing and flying off
beyond the roar of the waves.

I am a demented wave thrown down on a reef,
instantly torn apart to reveal the explosion of light.
The pieces gather up to form
a contemplative surface, a rising and falling mirror for our gaze.

I am the petrel in the branches of sunlight.
I am the fish that melts in the sea.
I am the red-eyed lighthouse staring into the hurricane.
I am the suffering sail gathering the power of the wind.
I am the anchor that longs for the drifting wave.

Moonlight embellishes white marble
now running with glistening tears,
slowly slowly slowly fading.

The blind man tears the sun apart.

Through the colours of the night sea
I flee towards the edge of darkness,
climbing one blue ladder ...

The Man and the Sea

Wind's fingers
Draw away the night curtain of the skylight.
The sound of the sun is dawning.
Clothed in white and flying out of the red-hued song,
A flock of gulls bump into sunlight, and the light tumbles down.

The island city moored in the glow of the sea.
The streets are strewn with traffic, tourists and pedlars
At the spot where sea and land embrace.
I bought a necklace strung with spiral shells and starfish,
A set of love stories.

This is a woman waiting between dawn and dusk.
This is a man setting out to sea when the tidal wave grows high.
This is a fish drowned at sea.
This is a quarrel between boat and anchor, wind and sail.
This is a mermaid's song forgotten by death.

How many people in waiting are lost by time?
How many people in pursuit die content?
How many people die safe in the nest?
How many people penny-pinching turn into mediocrities?
How many beautiful things refuse to be claimed by Death's memory?

When the fantasy leaps up among the pebbles,
Shattered by the waves,
A woman born in a seashell is walking towards me.
Her hair styled by a typhoon.
Her lips pressed wet with whales' kisses.

Rubik's Cube

You shrug off the babble looking gorgeous on you,
In tears, bid farewell to the fairy tales in the sunset
We encounter each other at a roundabout
The World, as a magic cube, appears so wonderful

Your tiny attic is the copy of the world,
It too can encompass everything
Man hides in his own Rubik cube,
Floating on the peopled sea

You say your eyes prefer the dark
The tiny Rubik cube only needs one little window
Then you fall in love with the black plane of the three-dimensional cube
Just leaving one white square

For the sake of an answer,
You start an endless quest.
In the small Rubik cube ripples the sound of your leafing through the pages
The pen in your hand draws out the flickering light of the oars' strokes

I am also contained in the world of this huge Rubik cube,
Seeking unity amongst the confusing colours within the small one
How could I steer your small boat like a Rubik cube?

Perhaps I am a stupid primary pupil
Between the small Rubik cube and the huge one
Making an equation without a solution
First, I and the small cube make up a known quantity
Then I build a bridge to the larger cube.

We are on a quest
We speak an ancient language

You untied the rope of thought and set sail to sea
To salvage the wreckage of your dream
I wish to be glue,
Your three-dimensional dream I hope to reshape
Hidden inside it the stories you heard, the toys you played with

You become rich
I am happy for you

When you can no longer bear the dark heavy solitude
I will be a ray of pure light,
Saturated with sunshine and oxygen,
Gazing through the window of your Rubik cube

Sometimes alone inside my own Rubik cube, I may pace up and down
Thinking about this sort of thing:
A girl uses seawater, starlight, reefs, storms
To write down her own log-book

You Predicted My Destiny

You turn around and wave to me.
The doors close like a camera shutter,
The tram moves on.

Your image surges in my mind,
A statue.

I turn away.
I'd like to take them home – this sky, the street, the tram.

You predicted my destiny,
That I would become a poet.
Since then your name has echoed in my blood.

I chose the black and cold volcano.
The crowded city bequeathed my space to others.
A man came who would reclaim
The mountainous wild manuscripts.

My bare feet bleeding,
As I tread the twisting snake-like path,
Print the earth with exclamation marks.
When the gold-helmeted sun was in the east,
I died by the fountain of myself –
Lavas of blood oozed from it,
My supply of ink.

When age is crawling on your forehead
And years have weathered your hair grey,
You will open your green diary,
Immersed in memory like light,
And recollect what happened then.

My poetry is sacred water beating in your ears:
A young girl rises from the watery light –
When you regret your beauty is beyond words,
perhaps then you will come to think of me.

Alleyway

I wade through the flow of midnight's church chimes
and enter an alleyway flooded with darkness.
A long narrow alleyway
rushes into my pupil, now grown large,
and my footsteps break the silence.

Lamplight surges from a half-opened door
melting the congealing night outside.
A sleepless girl in red
stands at the doorway beneath a magnolia tree,
violet flowers burn at tips of branches.

The sound of footsteps penetrates the deep alley.
I see the girl but I do not stop to talk.
I am a drowning man clinging to a piece of wreckage
drifting on black waves.
I draw the heavy night into my lungs, then exhale.

A lilac tree with a crown of white flowers
standing by the road
like a grey old man
who raises a shaking hand to point me the way.

Words in the spring breeze rock the light of wisdom.
The tread of footsteps
like the weary sound of splashing water,
shattering the stagnating night.
Perhaps it is a dead-end.
I feel dawn creep up
to look in through the window of my soul.

Voice

As soon as we leave the tunnel of our birth,
even before our bodies are cleaned of blood,
we all cry out, and those sharp cries
are the first signs of our talent for speech.
Later, we escape in many directions, and our voices
are lamps of fire in the rain, which fly up
looking for their own lines of light,
as flocks of birds rush through the trees
or birdsong falls along forest paths.
That is how our voices mingle with air.
Who can forbid something so natural?

World, we must have a talk about this.
We don't need any language to do it,
just to look at each other.
Nature's a womb not a refrigerator,
our voices which are spacious as the sky,
must not be frozen in us or we die.

Door

Within memory, snow fall.
Night
Whitens.
Frozen is the red handkerchief you fastened to the door
Like a flower sipping yesterday's
Pure sunlight.
The red handkerchief must be tired,
Leaning on the panel of the door.
A weary flag, in the wind.
Wood palings look about them
In the pure land of my heart.

Morning. The sun in the east
In a warm tone
Reads
Lines of love verse
Left on the snow-spread paper.

My love, let's walk out of
Memory's sky.

For you, I will create a garden
On the snowline.
In another world
Flowers open in the snow.
The flag calls over the skipping sunlight.

You left,
The door is closed.

I walk out of memory's snowstorm.

Night dresses the garden's silence
In black.

When sunlight flows down,
Packed snow thaws in the garden.
The fall of footsteps echoes in the distance.
On the doorstep, there may be a girl
Who fastens a maple shaped handkerchief,
Opened once to autumn frostbite.

And then knocks on the door.
Surprised, she sizes up what's hidden in the house.

Who Are You?
for Stephen Spender

I am a baby of premature delivery.
I am a genius who died before the age of thirty.
I am a child born inadvertently before the invention of contraception.

I am a devoted son now abandoned.
I am a young girl cherishing my virginity but raped.
I am a virile young man now castrated.
I am a loyal lover now betrayed.
I am the boxer pole-axed to the cheers of the spectators.
I am a vagrant leaning under moonlight against reality's wall.
I am a poet who detests hypocrisy now slandered by it.
I am a martyr adoring the sublime now buried by it.
I am a senile man, alone, staring with dull eyes at a setting sun.
I am beautiful blood gushing out from a body.
I come from contingent birth,
walking toward inevitable death.

I am severed ears still wanting to listen to good news.
I am a mouth venting suffering but gagged by a wall-like hand.
I am a severed nose still wanting to smell roses.
I am an unrequited lover expressing love with a torn-out tongue.
I am a pair of hands with amputated fingers holding my beloved.
I am legs trudging across snow enduring fractured bones.
I am a corpse that burned itself because it contracted cholera.

I am a matchstick struck then thrown away.
I am a liqueur glass shattered by a drunk.
I am a balloon rising over people's staring heads.
I am the remains of firecrackers lit by children, hated by streetsweepers.
I am a football writhing in pain under a player's foot used to decide who wins or who loses.
I am a lover's token taken by a thief.
I am a dog who saved his master's life dying from his gun.
I am the grapes of wrath which foxes could not reach.

I am a cloud men cursed but bringing timely rain.
I am an albatross fallen among the crowds of the marketplace.
I am the shoulders holding up the railway so that trains may pass.
I am the ordinary decorations of eternal space.
I am the grave goods of time.

I am a frayed rope, cursed by people who used it to tow their boat.
I am a piece of wreckage on the beach to which the drowning clung.
I am a mast broken by the sail's need.
I am the conversation between the sailors and tidal wave.
I am the conch shell, innards scooped out, now blowing a fisherman's song.

Who are you ?
I am I.
I am exactly what I am.
I am I.
I am just the thing I am.
I am I.

To C.J.

I

The wind is narrating cooling fairytales.
One ring of invitation after another blossoms within the snowflake.
The telephone line leads my words towards you,
"Look how those silver sounds are piling up in the wood".
You say I am a wisp of some romantic breeze.
Memory collapses and grazes your palm,
The bat-like debris falls and covers your dream.
The wood, bewildered, heaves yellow sighs.
Wind and snow wrapped in night freeze all human trace,
The dark hands of night muffle the earth.
At such a moment,
the falling snow is a group of innocent and untainted children.
Why don't we tread in the fall of such footsteps?
Look for the sun conceived in the womb of nightmare.
Have faith, on this land twitching with pain.
A morning song can be born from there.

II

The line of vision meets the outline of the shore.
So believe we are waiting and are being waited for.
We step out from among memory's ruins,
Struggling out of knots of the past.
At last, head towards the sea.
May the setting sun kiss away anxiety from the face.
May the sound of the waves rub away noise lingering in the ear.
Footprints on the beach are following a pair of snuggling shadows,
To wish farewell to the past.
Lean your head on my shoulder and start to cry.
Why does the pen you gave me, filled with inspiration, always pour out
                                            melancholy poems?
In the distance the golden wild flowers hint at a new season.
At this hour why don't we hold each other in close embrace?
Let the wind, a limpid handkerchief dry your tears.
The cloud is a navigation chart suspended above the sky.
The blue drum roll of the waves heralds a long voyage.

A Consultation

There is something wrong with my sight,
I cannot see clearly into the distance.
I go to my doctor and my doctor says:
"You have made a long journey through the night,
your eyes are full of darkness,
I fear that is incurable."
I realised the truth in his words.
Terror had broken into my eyes.
My memory is ransacked by thieves
and howls through my teeth with pain.
Those crooks are swinging from my every nerve.
It seems to me that eyes are envelopes
and make good cells – I seal mine tightly shut
and tell the doctor, "Please let me sleep."
I ask him to write out a prescription for death.

Birthday Card, 1990

When the winds of time have brought us the song we have forgotten,
Those words emerging from the memory glimmer again.
Love beans sown in the heart whisper that they want to grow.

In the Bathroom

Lying in the bath,
I am hungry for the world outside.
Suddenly you push the door open and come in.

I watch the electric light flirting with the steam.
Terror sweats from the pores of my skin,
Trying to seep through the bathroom glow.

My young body soaks in the frothing of dreams,
Past desires can still be seen.

Now my flesh is your food,
Your gaze brushes my deadened nerves.

I remember our first time,
I suspected there were others waylaid in my body,
Competing for the pleasure of my first night with you.
Time's terror hid in my foreskin.

You were the waiting instrument,
But I could not make you sound.

In penitence, my penis hung its head

I come back from that night long ago.
You have already left the bathroom.

Learning a New Language

Voice is a cluster of butterflies flying into memory.
Phonetic sounds leave a trace on the muscle.
Body temperature is a form of language.
My love, do you remember my touch?
Language is a kind of action.
My body has remembered you securely.

October, 1991

Words

I live within words,
Looking for ways to clothe ideas.
Words are a landlord
I sell myself to
And pay him rent.

I live within words.
When they fail me and I want to escape,
Words are a gaoler,
Who forces himself on me.
I am fighting a voice in every pore.

I live within words,
Words loiter inside my head.
When I don't feel like sleeping with them,
They rape me,
They dance in glory and in malice
Kicking up the dust of voices.

I live within words,
Words swim into my head.
When, out for revenge,
I try to destroy this house of words
Suddenly it turns amiable,
And makes friends with me.
We run away together to another house.

Does my landlord still want me as his tenant?

Chance

I died the very moment I was born,
I fell asleep as soon as I awoke.
How many of us find that tiny crack
And so escape a life we didn't make?

Discovery

It is not difficult to live in yesterday and tomorrow,
The difficulty is to live in today.
Spending today and observing the two ends of time,
Suddenly I am further and further away from today.

25 November 1990

Boarding the Boat of Death Half Way

Memory is a shattered vase.
New life will not be born from this jagged wound.
Only when eyes become wounds that do not heal
Will people learn the way to peace.

I am suspended head down inside the womb,
The self-sacrifice of a Mother.
Blood spatters the four walls of memory.
I swear I could recognise the colour of blood
Even before I was born.

This night my small coffin-like room
Lies abandoned in a corner
On the sixteenth floor of a tower-block.
The books which will go with me to the grave
Piled one on top of another,
Climb towards the ceiling,
Repeating words I have grown tired of.

With the blade of reason I slit
The blood vessels of my body.
The walls of books keel over.
The pale scattered pages are faces
Struggling in dark blood.
Asleep in my coffin I drift away on the night.

Memory is a landscape reflected in a cracked mirror.

The boat of death breaks through the changing scene.
The crash startles the soul from sleep
Clutching fragments of the world,
It bursts out of the nailed coffin,
And seeks the shelter of another vase.

Memory has a further chance to reassemble itself.

Desire Hotel

1

Desire is a hotel,
Man should he live there will grow wings.

2

The snares of dazzling stars,
Set round the earth where there is water.

3

When the sun rises from its bed of clouds
Prostitutes become true virgins;
The clocks turn to a heap of rubbish.

A Prayer

Close the book,
as night closes the clamour of the day,
let peace fall.

Through the railings of eyelashes,
you pass the bloodshot barrier
and you enter me.

I See

I see the sky crystallised into space.
I see the state of mind indifferent to fame.

I see the blue element of the sea filling the fish.
I see my life saturated with melancholy.

In the evening, I see stars struggling out of the cloud and mist.
I see the place where I long to live.

The Unfamiliar Customs House

Nightmares waylaid me. I could hardly make a declaration to the customs officer. I had become a smuggler, dealing in nightmares. I was once again in exile.

When I took up my pen for the first time to write poetry I felt exiled from the ordinary world; then I was only a teenager. My exile was a voluntary one.

The night in London became damper. Sound flutters its wings hovering in the air. The lighted cigarette in my hand is like a sleepless eye.

The sky of the square in my mind seems to me still like a bloody, messy wound.

My frozen tongue has come alive. I want to speak.

The way I came is broken by the wind; the way back is muddy with anxiety. Paths beneath my feet run in all directions in the moonlight.

It is in that home where my childhood is stored. The mirror has forgotten its owner. Nobody there will turn on the table lamp to lift up the night. Books in the bookcase still have my fingerprints, which have gone cold between the pages. The hanging lamp no longer tenderly gazes down at the bed. The dust of time has covered all the nightmares and all the love. The windows which let in sunlight have gone blind. Is there any green mould secretly crawling over the uncarpeted floor?

In another place, Mother, through her glasses, fixes her eyes on the only photo of myself as a child, expecting my mischievous footsteps.

I want to go back, I must go back. The way swallowed by night has not yet come into sight. Night is like soft rocks blocking my way back. Let the rock of the night crash into me.

I want to go back. I want to go back home. But where is my home?

When I intrude into another country, an unfamiliar customs house appears before me. It is the yellow earth of my home, which receives me. I become buried, as it were, by the warm yellow colour? I can slumber soundly.

The nightmare has been detected and confiscated by the customs officer.

A Day Within Days

China, you are my sodden nightmare.
How I yearn to escape from the swamp of your mouth.

China, I shall leave you for now.
You possess me.
I am encircled by the shadow that is cast down by myself.

I have finally left you.
You have sneaked up to the dream cave of my night.

How I long to go on writing poetry.
To make my imagination thaw,
Let me feel my cells swimming as fish again.

China, you are my nightmare.
You lull the children with gunshots and a caterpillar of tanks.

History is bleeding as we pray.
The executioner's time has not grown leaner.

In the dark, tree fingers stretch to the night sky to be snapped by bullets.
Tonight, salt crystals of the moon have not surfaced to fall into hollow wounds.
They could have prevented the flesh from decay.

Those valleys of the throat are crammed with different shaped words,
Pushing upwards tenaciously with the strength of breathing.
Strings of lies have become zippers of the shrouded dead.

China, you could not cleanse these wounds
With the river of your tears.

Alive, you force man to fight man, man to trample man.
Dead, you command one to press down on another, one to pile up upon another.
Why have you produced so much hatred?

The leaves of light are drifting down in corrupted wind.
The sun is a drop of blood splashed on grey paper.

I can never leave you.
I make love to you in my dream.

I saw you giving birth to me.
In turn, I gave birth to a wanderer,
Who could never leave China.

China, I want to sing.
I do not need to mark my name on the song.
You will recognise it is me who is singing, China.

China, I want to make love to you.
But I learnt that you are ruthless, a woman without sex.

You forbade me to ever fall in love (you said that was the privilege of the bourgeois).
You only allow me to love those leaders whom I get bored with at first sight
(It is a pity that so far I have not had a homosexual inclination).

My testicles swell up, and that makes me suffer.
My sperm blows up like rock and roll.

Those hoping to become pregnant are still waiting.

The breathing of the wind blows out the lamps.
Dreams settle,
The island of white bones looms.

I would go to the execution ground where my father was killed twenty years ago.
He was sending his ideals wrapped in those transparent gunshots –
Three bullets pelted through his head –
And I inherited his suffering.

On this day, I lean against the head of the wind.
White bones beneath my feet are turned to pebbles.
Crows are flocking in my thinning hair.

The past like a puddle of water fills my wound,
The wound where I seek my image.
The mirror reflects the bruised sky over Tiananmen Square.

From dusk of the twentieth century, I go back to dawn of two thousand
    years ago.
From the dawn of two thousands years ago, I return to the dusk of the
    twentieth century.

Lao Zi realises that his theory of "a small warless country of inhabitants",
"To make emptiness in each heart, to weaken ambition, to keep the people
    from knowledge and desire", has been plagiarised and distorted.

He recites the scripture of "The way that can be named is not the
    permanent way,
The name that can be called is not the permanent name",
Files a charge in the People's Court against Mao Zedong.
As a result, he is condemned to death for libel.

Zhuang Zi waking up from his dream of the butterfly is accused of
    "escaping reality".
He is obliged to price his imagination and take it to the free market for sale.
Poets and philosophers who have abandoned writing for business
Don't even bother to look at his offering.

Confucius without a diploma, unworthy of promotion, has to enrol at the
    Open University.
However, he is expelled by the school party committee
For promoting the idea that one must "establish others as well as oneself,
Wish them success as much as one's own".

Qu Yuan is denounced in a correspondence, his collection of orange pips,
Stolen by plain clothes police,
Is sold as far as Siberia by speculating government officials

And as he sanely sings a song of tribulation,
Throws himself into the troubled memories of the Miluo River to feed the fish.

Li Po, the loner, is floating in the air,
Refusing to be present at the banquet hosted by the United Front Ministry,
Is put in a strait-jacket,
Drinks Maotai with the colour of clouds.
And plunging into his own cup of wine
Drowns, embracing the moon.

Tu Fu leaning against the smoke of the great battle-fires of the real
                                        estate developers,
Sings in his wall-less cottage to warm the poor.
Here he lies dead of cold in his hovel,
A promise from the office to be rehoused still hidden in his pocket.

Wang Wei becomes a monk,
In the midst of the silence he lights incense in the remote, densely
                                        forested mountains,
And becomes a matchmaker for sound and colour
He suddenly gives up his monastic robes,
And goes to Beijing to open an international marriage agency.

Mao Zedong invites a private tutor to study the Book of Changes,
But he makes up sentences like, "the more one knows the more reactionary
                                        one becomes".
Overnight idiots become professors.

Mao Zedong lies in his transparent prison, serving his sentence ad infinitum,
Visitors look at him like a monkey,
To see how he continues to invent hate and strife.

He calls Stalin, Rocha, Ceaucescu, Honecker and Castro
To an enlarged meeting of the polit-bureau,
Deciding to expel Gorbachev from the Party.

Deng Xiaoping is lucky,
Qi Gong Masters have kept him half alive; dozing he plays bridge.
God decides not to bestow peace upon him,
Letting him neither rise to Heaven or fall to Hell.

Jiang Zemin erects a "Mao Zedong circus" on Tiananmen Square.
He appoints himself as the head, singing, playing wind, string and percussion
                                                             instruments,
An outstanding clown.
Chaplin insists that he's not right for the role.

Sartre and de Beauvoir decline the invitation to attend the review
Of the Second Cultural Revolution parade.
Instead they decide to get married on Tiananmen Square and invite all the
                                   Chinese students to attend their wedding party.
The Ministry of Security tries to persuade them to leave
As soon as possible for Hong Kong for their honeymoon or risk being kidnapped.

Li Peng's brain has had another break down,
Top Party secrets have been leaked again.
Again he has declared martial law on the whole country.
Very soon he is infected by a sexless being with Aids,
Whose tongue had to be transplanted.
Exhausted by the chase, just another anonymous victim on the wanted list.

China, how did I ever cut the umbilical cord, to impose exile on myself?
China, how did I become a rebel, to be banished by you?
China, how could I become a dissident, and not be tolerated by you?

From dusk of twentieth century, I go back to the dawn of two thousand years ago.
From the dawn two thousand years ago, I go back to the dusk of the
                                      twentieth century.

I remain puzzled by a question:
Those in power in China today, are they really Chinese?
I turn this in my mind over and over again.

Leafing through the history of China,
I can find no sovereign, of any dynasty,
Who imprisoned his subjects, made them his hostages
To trade with other states to his advantage.

The innate right to live,
Those in power sell it dear to their own people,
And would like them even to shed tears of thanks for the bestowal.

They say that human rights are not applicable to China.
Does this mean that the Chinese nation is inferior to other human races?
Why do those in power discriminate against their own Chinese people and
                                                          create such inequality?

They say that the world standard weights and measures will not be allowed
                                                              to apply in China,
So they may sell the people short.

I remain puzzled by the question:
Those in power in China today, are they really Chinese?
I turn this in my mind over and over again.

Who reigns over China?!

When the world has turned into one village,
I hope the avenues and lanes of China can lead to any corner of the world.
Freedoms are no longer luxury goods, which the people have to fight over
                                                                to purchase.
People no longer live simply in order to survive.

Who reigns over China?!

1994

Valediction

As I wait, illness makes me cherish every serenity.
Words still squirm inside my throat.

I will the words, 'I love you', into her mouth,
her breast risen, riverbank formed, my glances swimming.

She spreads her legs and invites me in.
I enter her to write.

She says: when writing, to live is more important than to write;
I say: when living, to write is more important than to live.

Our children are being noisy in the next room.
She: let them snip off a few of your poems,
    let her know how to choose her clothes,
    let him begin to think of how to think.

Poets say that imagination is a kind of reality;
one makes a home of mirage when disaster calls.

The past falls when it leaps up to the future,
death could not forgive me for being a poet.

I am the loneliness of a latticed window,
despair will not be anticipated by hope.

Every day is the last day,
tonight I invite myself to attend my own funeral.

Night is the silence of earth,
bury me.

Every moment is a last moment,
now I invite myself to be present at my own funeral.

Night is the weightlessness of earth,
entomb me.

The willow tree unfastens its green hair braid,
night cascades like a lover's black hair,

it caresses the bald headstone of my tomb.

At daybreak my bloodstream becomes a fire
burning, I am rainbow-hued and drained to nothing.

Words are a gleaming river in the night,
an elegy.

All children who read poetry are my own dear children.
Their voices are like dawn breaking over darkness.

Children I am back with you.

Listening to Chinese Music

1

A wood turns yellow in the autumn's breath,
Man and tree have discarded their clothes.
The space in the mouth is frozen,
A crack within sound.
The lips of the drowning
Still form the shape of words.
Spring
Leaps over winter's fence.

2

Raising a wine glass,
And asking the sky:
The sky is a blank page,

Can I write poems on it?
At this moment,
The music slows down — rest.
Silence.
A wall emerges within the track of thought,
A one-way train to Heaven
Selling only returns.
I step on to the train and leave.

Only One Way

The mirror is deep without end,
One cannot be drowned in it.

In the mirror,
I chance to meet
Myself.
I bump into myself.
We say in one voice,
"I am sorry"

The mirror is deep without end,
One can be drowned in it.

Insomnia

In the bedroom
The light is still on.
I am waiting for sleep to arrive.
The light will go out.
Night is water seeping through the window pane.
The head, which has gulped the sleeping pills,
Is being scorched by ideas one after another.
An explosion
Waits
To enter darkness.
The light within death,
The distinction between day and night has gone.
Fear is dispersed.

Standing at the Doors of Dusk

Standing at the doors of dusk,
I open words.
I see
darkness amid the silence.
The world emerges,
a man writes
with mutilated fingers,
the square in his mind is empty.

Bring your hands together,
move to a safe place to pray,
sprinkle water on silence,
watch the voices of light expanding,
now rip up that very silence.

The doors of the world
unlock —
thousands of imprisoned lives
flee in the wind of evening,
I hear the banging doors.

Instantly I shut the doors again,
and find the pursuing words
have already been decreed.

At Hawthornden Castle
for Pamela Egremont

In the hollow silence of the castle,
I sit at my desk and listen to my breathing.

In the morning, birdsong and the smell of green grass freshly cut
Follow the flow of river down the glen.
At midday, I pray you, stroke my forehead Sun.
At evening, let me believe the stars have something late to tell.

Memory projects my inner storms onto white paper.
Imagination reveals what's hidden under heaven.
Thank you.
You make me able to hear once more the scratching of my pen.

If I get tired,
I leave the castle and grow into a tree between earth and sky.

If any passers-by look me up and down,
Not a word, I'll say.

If I happen to turn into a tree in someone's head,
I'll then begin to whisper it away.

This Poem
for Warwick Gould

Before this poem reaches fullness
Filled inside with darkness,
The poet chooses words from the dictionary in his head,
As torches to light what lies ahead.

Without making the emergency exit in the sentence,
The defenseless poet walks from one line to another;
One moment he faces the danger of adventure,
The next he feels secure in the structure.

The corridor within the poem fills with light,
Readers walking by, observe it with delight.
This poem is on the point of its completion,
Readers swiftly abandon the final lineation.

The poet is locked inside the poem.

Liu Hongbin was born in 1962 in Qingdao, China. He worked as a clerk, teacher and journalist in China and was frequently harassed and questioned by the police for his literary and political activities. Four of his poems were posted around Tiananmen Square in 1989 during the events leading up to the massacres; he fled to London in the same year. In 1992, he began writing a PhD thesis in literature at the University of London and has since worked as a freelance journalist, lecturer and visiting research fellow. Attempts to return to China to see his mother resulted in expulsion in 1997 and detention in 2004; he is banned from returning. He is the author of two previous collections of poems, *Dove of the East* (hand printed in 1983 and circulated privately and secretly in China) and *An Iron Circle* (Calendar, 1992).

'Liu's luminous, hard-hitting poems expose isolation, psychic states pushed to the brink.' *The Guardian*

'(He) has continued to compose in his own language and has actively promoted contemporary Chinese literature in the West. Poetry has always been his chief love.' *Index on Censorship*

'Beautiful ... Liu Hongbin belongs to a very ancient Chinese tradition which insists that one of the chief duties of poets is to bear witness: often a more vivid impression of the mute miseries of the poor and the iniquities which caused them is to be gained from poems than from the writings of historians.

'What runs through all these poems ... is the unswerving dedication to his art, the obsessive interest in words.

'This book's translations by the English poets ... should give English-speaking readers the best idea of his poetry they are likely to get short of mastering the Chinese language themselves.' *David Hawkes,* Sinologist, Emeritus Fellow of All Souls College, Oxford.